CONCRETE & JUNIPER

CONCRETE
& JUNIPER

JOHNNY NO BUENO

CONCRETE & JUNIPER

CONCRETE & JUNIPER

JOHNNY NO BUENO

For my actual friends.
If you have to ask whether or not that includes you, it
probably doesn't.

Real recognizes real.

HƎLL PЯƎSS
UNIVERSITY OF HELL PRESS

This book is published by University of Hell Press
www.universityofhellpress.com

© 2020 Johnny No Bueno

Cover and Interior Design by Vince Norris
www.norrisportfolio.com

Published in the United States of America
ISBN 978-1-938753-36-7

TABLE OF CONTENTS

ACKNOWLEDGMENTS

"The Violence Given Me" was originally published by *Nailed Magazine*, June 2013.

Nothing in this book is factual.
Everything in this book is true.

"This is for the hard men who want love but know that it
won't come."
—Anis Mojgani, "Shake the Dust"

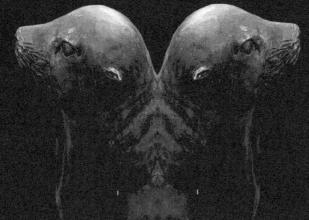
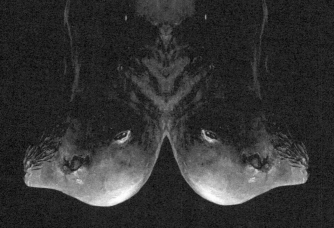

THE ONLY HOME I HAVE EVER KNOWN: PART I

PROLOGUE

Autumn always reminds me of heroin, hardcore, and the Seals. Somehow, I have always discovered the things I would later use to define myself in the fall. My first hardcore show was 7Seconds in September of 1996. Originally, I had only heard the name 7Seconds in punk 'zines, but I needed a full immersion. I suited up in my buddy's Dead Kennedys shirt and barreled into the pit like my hair was on fire as the consented violence of the mosh pit wrapped its gnarled limbs around me in its tattooed embrace. In direct opposition to the straightedge lifestyle of the vocalist, Kevin Seconds, I shot heroin for the first time one month later. Again, I needed full immersion. All of my rock star heroes and the "cool kids" I met while living on the streets of Portland were all shooting dope. After a seven-day meth binge, I asked my buddy Devil if the heroin he was cooking up would help me sleep. He drew up ten units of the black gooey substance and shot me up. You can guess the rest from there. But my life at the Seals started four years before that.

In 1992, I was in a foster home. I was unable to live with my alcoholic father, and my mother's home was a quiet Nagasaki unknowingly waiting for an atom bomb of my juvenile delinquency and rising penchant for violence to drop. I was interned at Joyce's house in Beaverton near the transit center awaiting whatever was to come of me. Joyce was a foster parent at the Boys and Girls Aid Society, always misheard as Boys and Girls AIDS Society. This got us foster kids odd looks and a whole lot of leeway. There must have been twenty to thirty of us spread out among various foster homes. Yet every weekday morning, all the foster kids would descend on the downtown Portland bus mall like a pack of starving hyenas on our way to the agency for school. We were loud and obnoxious, gleefully taking advantage of our hour or so free from the watchful eye of foster parents and social workers. While downtown, we would bum cigarettes. Some would buy drugs. The boys would desperately flirt with the female clients—and anything else that seemed to have bloomed into puberty.

One morning as I got off the bus at SW 5th and Yamhill, while looking for some random stranger to give me a cigarette, I saw punk rockers for the first time. There were three of them. One had a pink mohawk barely escaping from underneath the hood of his sweatshirt pulled down tightly to keep out the autumn chill. Another punk was tall with a green mohawk charged into spikes. He wore a heavily decorated leather jacket, complete with studs and "MENTORS" painted across the back. He also wore knee-high Doc Martens combat boots. White laces contrasting the nicked, scuffed-up matte-black of the leather boots made a barred pattern up his shins. I could barely make out his camouflage shorts underneath a quilt of crass and unreadable patches of what I assumed to be punk bands. The third was a chubby girl who wore two-inch blue suede creeper shoes, a tight red plaid skirt, and a pink mohair sweater. She had two mohawks, which I later learned were called bi-hawks, dyed in a leopard print pattern.

I was twelve years old. This is the first time I had ever seen real punk rockers, anywhere other than television. I was enamored instantly. Something about these three teenagers told me that they didn't have to worry about people hurting them. They sneered at every person who looked at them a split second too long. They mocked the police as the cops stared at the punks from their squad car. They screamed outrageously offensive slurs at those coming and going from the Meier & Frank department store across the street. They were self-sufficient and demanded respect mainly due to their ability to reject normality and docility. They had a little radio with them. The music that was wailing from the boombox, if you could call it music, sounded like tattooed-faced banshees come to wreak havoc on the innocent pedestrians during their sad, docile morning routines.

I also took notice of the spot where they were perched. Over the next couple of weeks, every morning when I got off the bus, I would look toward the Seals to see if they were still there. Sometimes they were, other times there was a whole separate group of punk rockers or skinheads. I took careful note of what the people at the Seals were wearing, who they were, what they were talking about, and what music they were listening to, on the rare occasion that they had a stereo. I needed to know everything about these people and this place. I needed to be a part of their world.

Bronze statues of animals surround Pioneer Courthouse, taking up the whole block between 5th and 6th Avenues, and Yamhill and Morrison. The Seals occupy the NE corner of the block. The Seals are bronze seal statues. There are three in the group. One lies on the red brick sidewalk, facing south. This particular seal is a favorite of passing families and children positioned at a perfect height for children to climb on top of, perfect for tourist photo opportunities. The second and smallest seal rises out of a fountain, facing north. This seal is the most ignored out of all of them. The third, the largest and most important, also rises out of the same fountain, but faces south gazing into foot traffic along Morrison's red-bricked sidewalk.

Beyond the Seals, Pioneer Courthouse is a looming presence of gray sandstone and black wrought iron fence. Somehow it always makes the already gray Oregon sky that much grayer. This seems the pivot of the entire city. All life seems to flow to and from Pioneer Courthouse. One could catch any bus, going in any direction, to anywhere public transit would take them. Pioneer Courthouse had become the central point of Portland, even though local citizens in 1869 criticized the architects for building the first US courthouse of the Pacific Northwest, as well as the second US Courthouse west of the Mississippi River, so far from the center of town. How was I to know that the Seals were to become the center of my life?

In 1994, while awaiting parole from juvenile lock-up, my father was murdered. After his murder, I had officially become an orphan. Upon being released from custody of Oregon Youth Authority, I was sent to a foster home. This woman, Reba, was the model of everything I came to hate in the world. She was an unattractive, short, busty woman who drove a Lexus, lived in a big house in the suburbs bought with inheritance money. Her husband, Larry, was a weak-willed cowardly salesman who would bow to her every drunken demand. I wanted to like him, 'cause when she wasn't looking, he would take the foster kids to Chinese food. He tried hard to relate to us, but I was disgusted by his lack of backbone. The daughter, Sarah, was a spoiled little brat, who would mock the foster kids for the freedoms or families they didn't have. I remember wanting to punch her every time I saw her pockmarked face.

Once, Larry had taken us golfing. I thought this was

kind of cool, but was embarrassed to be seen with these horrible, demanding people. On the ninth hole, I was getting ready to tee off. I lined up my shot and swung. However, on my forward stroke, Sarah popped her head from behind a slight hill. This startled me, and I tried to pull my shot, as she was really close to the trajectory of my stroke. But pulling only lined her up perfectly and the ball slammed right into her forehead. She began bleeding from a grotesquely large knot that instantly formed. At that same instant, she started screaming. I can't recall ever being so pleased with such a near-fatal mistake. It was all I could do to keep from laughing, which Larry noticed and was not happy that I took so much pleasure in having just hurt his little girl.

During my short stay, the house was being remodeled. An extension was being built next to the garage so the foster kids could live there, rather than take up precious room in their lovely house. Everyday, my foster brother Nolan and I, would come home from school where we would find a list of chores to do. This list was made up primarily of cleaning up after the remodeling, and then washing all of her dishes that had piled up during the day of her recovering from the prior night's drunken partying. Most nights, she went to the local casino and gambled. She would tell us about her "system" for winning on slot machines. I always found myself wondering, "If she won so much, why did we only ever eat macaroni and cheese or Hamburger Helper?"

I would sneak cigarettes and fortified wine on the roof at night, thinking about what my life would come to now that my father was truly gone. Was I actually expected to live out the next four years of my life under the care of people who just saw me as a way to pay the bills? This family had no interest in my well-being; this was clear. Now I was a ward of the state—another file to push around until they didn't have to place me anywhere.

So, I ran away. There was one place on this Earth that I still understood as safe, or home. When I got to the Seals, I sat down and wept in the autumn wind and rain. I had only ever seen homelessness on television. I thought destitution was a myth.

5TH & MORRISON

The rain never lets up,
yet never washes away the stench
the vomit that seems the stain
of our presence on 5th & Morrison.

The cleansing odor of hot wet concrete
would open our pores
as the click of high heels
& the blurt of car horns
would seance the whiskey out of us
like the forgotten spirits we had become.

We taste blood & body odor
sitting as righteous as indignant punk
would allow, lulling our feet comatose,
listening to the ambulance music
& the choir of breaking glass.

A bronze seal statue is our only center,
as it lords over addled minds compliant
like whitened knuckles of a hope held too tight.

The rain never lets up.
We only notice this
because we're always left
searching the puddles at our feet
for our reflections,

praying we are
not yet invisible.

NICKLE SKY CRIES

This tightening necktie season,
all concrete & juniper, leaves
us all a bit shaken up. Pigeons
perched atop blue-gray sandstone
roof seem motionless. Yet a head
jolts into view, as a wing twitches.
Rain clouds hover beyond
the flock, as if painted
with blinders on & a hankering
for Bohemia. The birds watch
as rats with backpacks,
with cellphones, with schedules
to keep, scurry back & forth
in their arbitrary & belligerent
existence.

                      Tree tops dip,
like a bad version of the shimmy,
like shiver, branches lurching
like do-the-twist, like the hills-
are-alive-with-music; not alive,
not dead. Flags erratic, like dubstep,
like overdose seizures, complete
with foamed lips in public bathrooms,
& the everything else. All of this
& everything, nothing more
than a black canvas, unusable,
through the lens of the malleable
& flammable. The omnipotence
of destruction is more than or
less than the gray
we all seem to bleed now.

BACKSPACE BLUES

for Backspace (RIP)

loneliness is a party gone on too long
or a conversation you don't want any part of
but desperately want to be heard
or a guitar solo in the wrong chord
or dance when your legs can't see the next step
or the last drop of a bottle

it's like being too old to get the inside joke
the rumble in your belly
even though you have had too much to eat
the connection you found
but not the words to make sure
it is the fear before the roller coaster
watching a young girl buy into the lie of beauty

the band you have heard
of but have never listened to
the doo-wop song you can't get
out of your head during karaoke
without the courage to get up & sing it
or getting to the end of the diving board
& realizing no one is watching
or not being able to pull
down the dusty photo album

I forget all of these
sitting across from
your morning coffee

THAT SAYING ABOUT NOT PICKING YOUR FAMILY

This gun is a surprise birthday present
from the archetype of so many orphans.
Cold. Hard. Such simple examples of why
my family still talks in circles. Still uninviting
to those actually affected. A daisy chain.
A spiral. The pain of jiggling a loosening tooth;
much more still-life picture-perfect fuck-yous
handed out annually like some stupid fucking banquet
while the pig twitches. Still alive. On the plate.
On its back. Legs in the air. Screaming.

MIGHT MAKES RIGHT

The hawk perches above the field
his collar of blue glinting violently
against the backdrop of gray green & brown.

Furiously with tense eyes
he searches for prey.

Ignoring his brethren of black crows
they are but birds, he seeks
the chilled blood of white-skinned rodents
meandering the hills and under rocks
carrying out orders of instinct.

This earth is a battle of necessity;
a holy war of immeasurable weight.

To carry out the divine task
that each bird is born for.

To feed. To be fed.

The prey he watches, their knowledge of his presence
gone, he sees them as a cancer of sorts
feeders who do not return the favor
to the land they are born of.

Scavengers
hideous beasts that must be fed upon
annihilated & destroyed

they have no purpose
they come not from noble blood

but are bottom feeders
surviving upon their capacity
to disappear into mediocrity & meekness

how could they ever understand
the heft of clouds, or how the wind itself
reaches out to them, & carries them upon
a throne made solely for their rage.

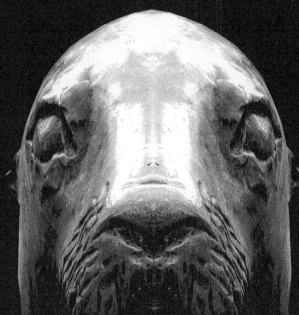

THE ONLY HOME I HAVE EVER KNOWN: PART II

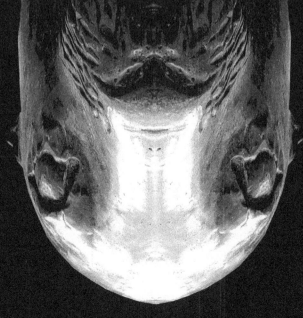

HONEY, I'M HOMELESS

This was the first time I fully understood, and experienced, *alone*. I had set out on my own, knowing no one, but I had my best interest in mind, regardless of what my case workers and parole officer told me. They just needed to place me anywhere. I was nothing more than unwanted cargo that needed to be put somewhere, at least until I had enough and did something to get myself locked up again.

But there I was at the Seals, my lifelong goal. Yet the only other person there was Sammy, the name I had given the bronze seal figure facing the sidewalk. I confided in him my fears, my tears, and my quickly dwindling hopes. It did not take much to convince me that no matter where I was going in life, no matter where I had been or what I had done, Sammy would always be there. Sammy would always listen and would never judge me. He would never pawn me off on a different social worker. He would never forsake me for anyone else. Sammy became my only friend. That corner became my only home.

I always sat to Sammy's immediate left, which is where I would meet most of whom I would later come to call family. Here I met the first lesbian couple I had ever known, Kade and Schitz. They took me on my first freight-hopping escapade to San Francisco. I met Devil, who gave me my first shot of crystal meth, which also happened to be my fifteenth birthday. I met Lucy, whom I would later date on and off. She killed herself the very day we last broke up. I met Damien, who was the first person I ever knew to die of a heroin overdose. I met Screw, Skunk, Vomit, Spit, Strawberry, Poopdick Chris, Wino Scotty, Evil, Rushin', Tomorrow, T-Dog, Ashes, Rufio,

Gutterpunk Chris, Ande, Jordan, Rotten, the Tweeker Twins, and hundreds of different train hoppers, squatters, junkies, drunkards, street thugs, punk rockers, skinheads, hardcore kids, goths, dropouts, degenerates, and other beautiful and detestable examples of American homeless and forgotten youth.

We used to sit at the Seals and panhandle drunk and/or strung out. To this day, one of my favorite pastimes is drunkenly accosting innocent strangers, demanding money we didn't need nor deserve. If we were lucky, we would offend someone just enough to make them think it would be a good idea to try to salvage their fading dignity by fisticuffs. At this we would all jump on the poor unknowing soul and inhumanely decimate any self-respect by beating him as badly as possible. In retrospect, it is rather worrisome what bored, forsaken, drug-addled, angst-ridden youth are capable of for the sake of entertainment.

At one point in my life, I had made it as far as the Yamhill Pub—the bar three blocks away. The cops were on to us. One officer, whom we had lovingly nicknamed Cup-Sniffer, would stop us and ask to smell our cups. He had become keen to our habit of opening cans of beer, dropping them into the bottom of paper soda cups, sticking the straw through the top of the can, and sealing the lid, so as to give the illusion of sipping on a to-go soda. Except we were never that slick, as we would all have cups from different fast food chains and convenience stores. He also took to smelling our Nalgene bottles, which were always filled with wine from a space bag.

Bars were always expensive but pints at the Yamhill were only a dollar. I opted for the more expensive option if it meant I was to be free and clear of the cops and another open container or drinking in public ticket. I remember one particular time when I was imbibing at my newly found watering hole, and two of the younger crew from my corner were calling for me. Still too sober to want to talk to Strawberry, I begrudgingly made my way to the door, as they were too young to join me in the bar. I was intrigued. As I made my way outside, away from the noise of a Merle Haggard filled barroom, they proceeded to tell me that there was a guy on my corner harassing the younger girls and threatening the boys. They were asking my permission to beat him up, as he may have been a friend of mine and they feared retaliation on my part. I have to admit, feeling like the Godfather of a street corner felt pretty good. Sure, it was one corner, and, sure, it was in dinky-ass Portland, Oregon, but wielding power over anyone, even if it took the face of fear, was quite a stroke to my often deflated ego.

Not completely sure I knew who they were talking about, I decided to place a coaster over my beer, and follow them up to the corner to see who was doing the harassing. As I neared the corner, I realized that there was no way that I knew either of the two casually-dressed men, so I reacted as any street corner lord would—with extreme prejudice. The tallest guy had his back to me, so I aimed straight for him. When I got directly behind him, I yanked the back of his shirt over his head, covering his face. Holding the shirt in place, I began wildly throwing haymakers into the spot where his face was. On cue, Strawberry and Black Ryan, called such because he wasn't Caucasian, grabbed the shorter of the two men and began trying to wrestle him to the ground. In the meanwhile, I had gotten the big guy to the ground. In a split second, Strawberry and Ryan had lost control of the smaller guy and I was put into a full nelson.

"We're off-duty cops," screamed the beer-laden breathed guy struggling to detain me.

"I don't give two fucks; not one for either of you," I retorted just in time to kick his comrade square in the nose with my steel toe Doc Martens.

The splatter of blood from his partner's face was enough to shock him and cause him to barely loosen his grip. I took the opportunity to drop, slipping out of his grasp, pivot, and land an uppercut to his jaw sending him spiraling into the side of the oncoming train. At this point, both men were knocked unconscious. There was a smattering of onlookers gathering. I yelled at the two of my younger friends to not ask me to fight their battles for them, before I ducked into the mall across the street, out the entrance on the opposite side of the building, onto the train, up to the next stop, across Pioneer Square, onto another train, down two stops, past the bleeding lumps and the two bike cops who stopped to assist them, and back into the Yamhill Pub.

A man must protect himself and his own. Years ago, we staked our claim to that corner. We must see to it and the people that inhabit it. Years may pass, people may come and go, but the corner remains. People came and went. Every week, we would get news that one of our own was dead or locked up. The Seals was a newsstand for some, and a message board for others. Shit, even the business professionals who knew our faces and sometimes even our names would ask us about certain people. If something was going on in Portland, the Seals was the place to find out.

One time, we had heard Wino Scotty was dead. Those of us who knew him put together a memorial service. When it came for the quiet slide show portion of the service, Scotty kicked in the door, shitfaced, waving the bladder of a box wine, screaming, "So I heard I was dead!" Some people were pissed, but we couldn't deny the humor of it all. The rumors were sometimes untrue. Most times, they weren't. Scotty died a year later of an overdose. We always claimed to know better than to shoot dope while drunk, yet that is how most of my friends died.

DIM THE LIMELIGHT

Put the bat down & pick up this Bible, son,

they said.

Put the bat down & pick yourself up,

they said.

Put the bat down & pick up this gun,

they said.

Put the bat down & pick up this cause,

they said.

Put the bat down & carry this cross,

they said.

Put the bat down, unburden your weight,

they said.

Put the bat down & carry with you peace,

they said.

Put the bat down & whisper this melody,

they said.

Put the bat down & remember this melody,

they said.

Put the bat down &

march to this tune (they said) walk to this beat
(they said) swing to this song
(they said) hum a few bars (they said) belt a
few out (they said) fall in line
(they said) do what your told (they said) might
is right (they said) two pairs of
footprints (they said) stacking bbs (they said)
walk the line (they said)
tow the line (they said) carry your weight (they
said) you're on your own
(they said) different (they said) out of line (they

said) delinquent (they said)
deviant (they said) criminal (they said) insane
(they said) mental defective
(they said) malcontent (they said) take it for
granted (they said) black sheep
(they said) apart from the rest (they said) fallen
angel (they said)
redemption (they said) rags to riches (they said)
see what we have done
(they said) one of the good ones (they said)
glad he's on our side (they said)

Pick up the bat.
Pick up the bat.
Pick up the bat.
Aim right;

swing.

THIS TRAIN, THIS HELL

The smoking car on an Amtrak hugging Canada
reeks of sulfur & the stench of failure.
This is divine comedy.

I shit my pants as we pull out of Spokane,
as we descend into the basin barren,
Idaho   Montana   Inferno.

Dope sickness swells in my gut.
Abandon all hope, ye who enter here.
A long way from relief; I just sit & smoke.

Unlike the first two poets to enter this grim place,
I cannot faint. The sleepless twitch keeps me stirring,
unable to find comfort in this hard chair.

Across from me is an unrepentant but kind woman
heading to Chicago to marry a woman she met online.
She fed me drinks from the bar car,
                              to take the edge off.

The wind rocks the cabin as two teens,
make like Lancelot & Guinevere, stealing kisses
from loved ones back home, leaving the rest of us
uneasy in the forever breeze.

Outside, the rain makes mud. I make believe
that this is for the mouths of Cerberus,
giving us passage. I almost got tossed to the wilderness
for a drunken outburst.

I make my way above from the dining car for scraps to eat.
A meal unfinished by a man asleep in his seat was taken
from my grasp by a conductor; jousting with my lack
of pocketbook, he accused me of not paying.

I find a syringe in the bottom of my bag. It is an angel's wand,
comforting me as I sunk into thoughts of *Dis* & how she left.
Finding courage, I break the needle. Medusa's hair,
cannot hold me forever. I am still far from free.

A conversation about God sparks up & is met
with vehement disdain, but I find it hard to disbelieve
in something I cannot see, as I am two days
into a journey that science could not fathom.

My body gives over to the agony. There is no buffer.
This boiling of blood, this fire, courses through me,
removing the remnants of slow suicide, I no longer
find any need to curse my existence as I fall
into the divinity of pain.

The train goes green with memories of the people I have
robbed,
the wife I left at home crying while I ran the city streets,
will this ever be made right? I am fetal on the rocking train car.

As I exit the train into the Boston night, nine hours late,
I make my way to a bench to sleep off this last night
& wait for my wife's morning arrival.
Unable to sleep, I stare into the eyes of Satan, the whole night.

Coming out of a daze, I see my wife; blue flower skirt,
cherry red Doc Martens, matching hair, I look into her eyes,
kiss her mouth, & realize, I have made it.

I descended & have arisen clean
like the poets.
   A chill comes over me.
      What purgatory awaits?

THE CITY SWEATS AS WE DO

The whistling taxi is a little overwhelmed. My darling,
we sit upon red bricks & stoops listening to rain
as it pours on to us & into us & out of us. The sidewalk
chalk
is slowly melting into the river that my street is birthing.

Like broken. Like water. Like riptide tsunami life
from between the parked cars of her thighs.
My city erupts into a hospital,
                                        & these buildings—
these buildings are nothing more
than the gowns worn by the ghosts

of The Everything the West prayed it could become.

BREASTPLATE

She has a tattoo, something about humility,
        across the expanse of her chest. They call
it a breastplate, tattoo above the breasts,
        reaching into the crevasse of cleavage,
bringing art & focus into an area
        any man can tell you needs none.

We sat that day in the park, watching her daughter
        run merry-go-rounds 'round the jungle gym,
a rather interesting contrast to the world we fought
        so hard to escape. The moment a brother realizes
that the girl across from him is no longer his sister
        but a woman, wild, wonderful, & fully aware.

Our survival against the odds, odds stacked
        upon us by a mother who never wanted such a title,
is not unlike her breastplate tattoo; loud, obnoxious,
        yet something agelessly cathartic & wonderful.
Just like the art highlighting cleavage.

THE EIGHTH PLAGUE

By the edge of the West, the wind blows,
full of sand. The moon howls her blues song;
the devil thorns of whipping stones
lie in bloody piles beneath her feet.

Locusts overtake everything
& she is left naked, in tearful prayer.
To lightning; we can only imagine
it is the grin of a vicious god.
By the edge of the West, the wind blows.
Just as Job sobbed, so does she.

Take them from this Earth, dear Lord,
remove from us the thorns under
our fingernails. We know not our crime

but know too well the cost.
Willing to pray, she pulls a gun
from the shifting sand, pulls the trigger.
The Earth drinks & is appeased.

SAILORS TAKE WARNING

+ + +

I remember my first memory as vividly as the midnight silence fills my basement apartment, reminding me I will leave this world just as I entered it—cold, wet, and screaming. The night sky was violet. I remember it was violet, because years later I heard the old rhyme:

> *Red sky at night*
> *sailor's delight,*
>
> *red sky in morning*
> *sailor's take warning.*

When I heard the old rhyme for the first time and remember thinking, *Well, what the fuck does violet at night mean then?* There never seems to be any corroborating nursery rhymes, songs, or archetypes for my experience.

That night, I stood in the middle of the street, holding my mother's hand. It was raining and cold. I think we were both crying, but I am positive my mother was crying. Between sobs, she screamed towards the house. I remember turning my gaze from her to the dirty yellow, dimly lit porch where I saw my father standing. So was his shotgun. It leaned against the frame of the door. The porch light gleamed from its maliciously grinning trigger. He was moving a large spindle we had used as a porch table. There was some kind of conversation, yelled back and forth between my parents, because of the distance and the rain—something about killing and something about dying. I am not sure if my father was talking about killing himself, my mother, me, or all of us. My mother pleaded with my father to let us get our clothes and use the phone so she could call *her* mother to pick us up. My father conceded.

As we entered the house, my father struck my mother, knocking her to the blood orange linoleum foyer floor. I don't know why I bent, losing sight of my father, but I bent nonetheless. As I neared her bleeding face, she whispered to me, telling me that I needed to get my father's guns, hide in the bathroom, and unload them. As my father entered the kitchen to take a drink, I grabbed the shotgun and raced upstairs. I cleared the stairs in maybe three or four leaps and bounded across the hall into the bathroom. I put the shotgun in the bathtub. I exited the bathroom for the closet across the hall. I opened the door and climbed the three built-in shelves to reach his two other handguns. I took them down, went back in the bathroom, and locked the door. I unloaded the guns as I listened to the screams of my mother getting beaten downstairs.

As I nervously fumbled with each gun, having no idea what I was doing, I found myself getting nauseous. The .44 Magnum Red Ruger gave me the most problems. As I realized that I might not be able to unload the moon clip, I started to vomit. I had to somehow unhook the revolver's cylinder from the chamber and remove the bullets, but I couldn't figure it out. Giving up, I cried. With vomit gurgling past my lips, in frustration I threw the pistol into the bathtub. Upon impacting the tub, the moon clip burst open. I eagerly scrambled for the bullets, piling them upon the bathroom counter. I now had to find something to do with them. I decided to try to brave the fire. I was going to gather the bullets into my shirt and run down two flights of stairs, past my father's ruthless and unending attempt to cripple my mother. I had to pull myself together.

Funny the things we learn, without any prior knowledge, when desperation calls, as if we inherently know exactly what to do in certain circumstances, if for the sake of survival. I shoved my fingers down my throat, making the bubbling vomit come to an all-out expulsion, ceasing the perpetual slow foaming of vomit past my lips. I tried to aim my face in the direction of toilet but didn't really care if the puke actually made it into the toilet or not. All the while, I kept an ear to the door. I needed to stay aware of the situation downstairs. As I wiped the last of my stomach's contents from my face, I heard that the fight had made its way into the kitchen. Assuming my father had chased my mother in there, it meant that he would have his back to me. I couldn't question it any further. If I didn't dispose of these bullets and try to get myself in a position to help my mother, we all might die.

I kicked the door open and in one fell swoop, cleared the first set of stairs. My father, hearing the impact of my feet hitting the ground not but five feet behind him but too drunk to move quick enough, just cocked his head, like a curious dog. I couldn't wait. Jumping down the last set of stairs, I ran though the family room to the sliding glass door.

At this point I could hear my father, "Where are you headed, Sean? You need to get the fuck to bed!"

Nervously, I fumbled for the latch, worrying about my father following me downstairs. When I got the door open, a voice came from the family room doorway, but it wasn't my father's. I glanced behind me to find my mother, barely able to hold herself up, standing there. If it weren't for her blonde hair, I would not have been able to recognize her behind the swollen lips, blackened eyes, or blood-smeared cheeks.

In a faint whisper she moaned, "I love you. Run."

I ran into the rain-filled night, and around the side of the house, throwing the bullets behind the dog house. Needing as much momentum as a little boy could gather, I turned around and I ran as fast as I could. As I neared the threshold from the back yard to the family room, I saw that my dad was inching his way toward my pleading mother, cowering in the corner. I aimed straight for him. I had no idea exactly what I was intending, but I knew I needed to try to stop him. As my five-year-old body connected with his, of thirty-six years, I felt a *give*. Everything went into slow motion when his boot grazed my shin. His feet had been knocked out from under him. I realized he was falling backwards onto the coffee table. So be it.

Ignoring my broken father and shattered coffee table, I walked upstairs to the phone and dialed 9-1-1. I told the operator that my mother was hurt and that my father couldn't move after falling down the stairs. I handed the phone over to my mother so she could give them the address. After she hung up, she called *her* mother. When the cops got there, I pretended to be asleep. I could hear the taking of photos and the asking of questions. Every five minutes, or so it seemed, an officer would open my door and check on me, as my heart would skip hoping he would not read *awake* in my fractured breathing. When my grandmother arrived, she walked through our front door. Ignoring the cops, my mother, my father, and walking straight up into my room, she scooped me up like a triumphant fireman exiting a burning building carrying a choking child. To this day, I still revere her as she was in that moment.

My mother and I moved in with my grandmother, but there was no way my mother could care for me financially. So, she brought me back to my father. He wore a back brace for many years after that, coupled with regular trips to the chiropractor and eating Doan's Back Pain medicine like candy. We never spoke of that night. I don't know if he ever forgave me. Perhaps not.

+ + +

Nine years later, on the morning of New Year's Eve, I looked out the window and saw a red sky.

Huh? I found that odd but went about the day as usual. After getting out from behind bars, there was really not much to do at a juvenile pre-parole work/study camp on holidays but play pool and ping-pong. I was waiting out the last two weeks before getting paroled to my father's house. Such a plan was not easily made.

Years growing up in my father's house put us at odds with each other. I had become a thief and a liar, and later a criminal. After my mother left, and after my stepmother left, I became the focus of my father's anger. Before getting locked up, the last time I had spoken to my father was when he picked me up from the police station for curfew. That night, he beat me worse than I had ever been beaten, or even witnessed. The next morning, I packed up my things, kissed my basset hound, Pippen, goodbye, stole a bunch of money, and left him a note promising to kill him if he ever spoke to me again.

My day included sneaking a cigarette in the shower when I could, daily observing my three canonical masturbation sessions, and betting porno magazines and cans of chewing tobacco on ping-pong and cards. Seeming it was a holiday, we were given special phone call privileges. I called my father's house.

When my father's new wife picked up the phone crying, I instantly angered, thinking he had started drinking again and was beating her. This would definitely jeopardize my parole. My stepmother asked to speak to my counselor. After handing the female intern the phone, I paced around the office, breathing strong deliberate breaths. I knew I was about to lose my cool and had to get myself as calm as possible. My counselor asked me to sit down upon hanging up the phone. Reluctantly, I sat. The moment she started talking, I got dizzy.

Your father has been killed ... his body ... naked ... gun shot ... abuse to his body ... stab wounds ... three days to identify his body ... your parole officer ... take you home ... home ... I'm sorry, that was insensitive ... tomorrow ... funeral on Tuesday ... Sean ... I am so sorry ... ...

One part of me told me to stay and listen; one part of me told me to run. I stayed as long as I could before running out of the office, screaming into the rain. As I inhaled fresh stormy breath, I fainted. When I opened my eyes, the sky was violet.

SUCH A HEAVY LOVE FOUND IN WELL-READ BOOKS

A gas-lit anthem waltzes
among dust particles
& olfactory nuances
between the shelves
of the dim bookstore.

Searching for a mirror among
dust jackets & redemption
enclosed by title pages & acknowledgments
but there is no escaping the bad boy poem
rattling between my ears.

*My first sin was a young American girl**

Like a first-time returned,
flip through frayed pages
of unexplained metaphor
about bricks & the history
wedged between them like mortar.

I find myself in the gray
spring morning, asking if this
is the story I have been trying
to find a voice for, all these years.

*& my first sin was a fear that made me [whole]**

Stumbling between words I don't understand,
the whole shelf feels as if it's leaning
in to crush me & within moments
for too much guessing, for too little help.

The whole bookstore seems to arch
up & over my head, watching my every step.
I want to run, to break open
twin glass doors & breathe
yet this familiar is not so easily ignored.

    *& she says, "Your first sin was a lie you told yourself"**

Standing here clutching the book,
clenching my eyes shut, sweating,
until light seeps in, until more room,
until less threat. Opening myself into it all,
I lean into her.
"What does this mean?"

*lines from Gaslight Anthem song, "The Navesink Banks"

SEX, LIGHTS, TAVERN

The sting of drywall between knuckle cracks in winter,
the over-head light bulb, the smell
of cooking heroin, over the noise of the jukebox,
& warm dry flatness of Budweiser swayed
to the tune of a Merle Haggard sawdust anthem,
or the Sex Pistols, either way it's Texas.

Either way, too familiar, unlike the softness
of a woman's gentle touch, or ravaging blood
from his back by chipping Lee Press-Ons
& never alluring badly dyed blonde highlights,
from girls who knew the buck of the rodeo
by the time they hit high school & have been
looking for a man to do the same for some years now.

NOW THAT SHE'S SOBER, I'M AFRAID SHE'LL LEAVE ME

While the mandolin yodels like a dying cat, the heart
skips & the throat jumps.
The coffee is too much & the catharsis too little, I am
heaving between drags of this cigarette.

The scribbles are droning on like bad metal; my feet
bare-knuckle box with each other.
Everything tastes like berries & the idiosyncrasies of
colloquial inflections are waltzing in time.

This is Thursday night, waiting for Friday's illusion of
something different,
the day after Wednesday's hopelessness; something I
forgot about long ago.

Lights & pens & teas are not enough to calm me down.
How many new neuroses will rise to the surface like
turgid corpses,

stinking up the neighborhood with its bloat & gas &
unsightliness?
The meetings are helping, but the gin is singing

                    singing
                          so sweet.

RESTLESS CHILD

Her scars are like cave paintings,
beautiful & austere, ageless surrender.
She couldn't box up the moment
like a photograph, so she wears it.
The dizzying fright of threat rings
like the blast of a whistle off wet pavement,
all sulfur & summer sweat. I took
her in, to keep her free from daggers
& pistols, but she wound up entangled
in me & I in her. The greatest mistake
I have ever made. When she sleeps,
I dare not crack open her fluttering eyes
by stirring. I never want her to wake
into the nightmare that our passion
was born from. I dare not wake her for fear

she will jump at the sound of my heart
breaking repeatedly against the walls
of my chest, every time she jumps at a sound.
She has no patience for innocence. How
can I tell her that every dream she will
ever have sleeps as she does, under healing skin?
I guess I will have to wait, until she finds
her way, back to the cavern of my arms
& paints herself into me.

THE VIOLENCE GIVEN ME

There is a river of blood unseen, but fueling the society in which we live. I just happen to be a boatman. I was born into it, baptized in it, and nourished from it my whole life. I hate it, but it is there. This violence is not something I want people to experience. I often find myself wondering how large my martyr complex is, but then again, such terms were created by mundane, privileged people, who lead mundane, privileged lives. You see, where I come from violence is a ballet. The cold inhumane streetlamps: stage lighting. Boomboxes and headphones: orchestra pit. We carry on in our universe so that the rest of the world can look upon us, and judge us: criminals, thugs, monsters, ruffians, gangsters, scum of the Earth. Orwell was right when he claimed that people sleep peaceably in their beds at night only because rough men stand ready to do violence on their behalf. My friends and I are the rough men and women of whom he spoke, standing ready to fight. We grew up at the end of a fist. It is what we know.

+ + +

Summer 1992

I tell the arresting officer to please call my mother instead of my father. My mother lives in Canby, the town I had come back to, to hang out with friends, the very same friends with whom I got picked up for curfew. It would be so much easier for her to come and get me, seeing she lives only blocks away, than it would be for my father who lives ten miles away. Plus, my father is drinking again and will definitely beat the shit out of me.

Every year throughout my life, my father had gotten more and more violent with me. It started as spankings, then flicks to the back of my ear. This progressed to smacks upside the back of my head, and on to kicks to wherever he could drunkenly land them. The last time my father had struck me it was an open-hand slap. I'm afraid this time it will be a full-on fist.

When the officer comes back into the room, I ask him who he called. He tells me that my father was on his way to get me. *I have to get out!* My eyes darting around the room for an exit. Of course, there are none, this is the police station. But what if I made as if I was trying to escape? I wouldn't get far. They would surely have to charge me with resisting arrest, eluding an officer, and attempted escape. I would be a run risk. They would have to take me to Donald E. Long Juvenile Detention Center, but I would be safe from my father. I guess I just have to sit and wait.

I can't tell you how much time has passed, but I can say that the second I see my father's whiskey-red face through the window in the steel door, all time slows down. He glances through the window and sees my face. His jaw clenches, and he walks into the room like an assassin walking out of the shadows and into a gun fight, all Clint Eastwood and ambient music. Every movement is fluid and purposeful. Even his swaying and intentional drunken gait seems to have its own rhythm. Just as his head crests the threshold of the door, he is called back by the officer. I hear, "Mr. Bowers, your son is scared that—" and the door closes.

This stupid fucking cop is telling my dad that I told him that my dad will beat me up. You have got to be fucking kidding me. This well-intentioned, yet ignorant, cop has just signed my death certificate. *Fuckfuckfuckfuckfuck!* I look at Holly next to me and tell her that if she doesn't hear from me in a day or two, to call the police. My dad will at least attempt to kill me. I just pray he isn't successful. My dad opens the door and holds it, head bent in shame. I get up to go with him, walking as slowly as possible, so I can cherish these last moments of life. I know too well that this act won't last long.

We walk in silence to the car. In silence, he starts the car. In silence, he starts driving. In silence, he turns the radio up. In silence, we edge our way out of town. In silence, he turns the radio off. No longer silent, the monster speaks: "So, I am going to beat you up, huh? I thought you were smarter than that. But, no. And now you are going to know what it is like to get beat up."

+ + +

Violence was given to me just as one might receive breast milk, from as close to the heart as any other human can be.

+ + +

Summer 1997

We gather in the park blocks of what will come to be called the Pearl District. Punks, skinheads, anarchists, street-corner hooligans—there must have been forty or fifty of us. The tension is thick as concrete. I'm chain smoking, trying to look as confident and together as possible. Some people are stretching, some are checking their weapons, some are lacing up their boots. Everyone is anxious. Bobby, the captain of Rat City Boot Boys, the local Skinheads Against Racial Prejudice (S.H.A.R.P) crew, cries out, "Alright, everybody gather around!"

Bobby gets us all in a huddle, or at least what could be thought of as a huddle. "Okay, most people know why we are here. White supremacist band West Side Bootboys are playing under an assumed name at the Lion's Den. They know, as does all of Portland by this point, that the further spreading of the white supremacist agenda will not be tolerated. This. Is. Rat. City. This. Is. Our. City. We have done away with asking. This is not a mission of diplomacy. So, if any of you are afraid of getting your hands dirty, possibly winding up in the hospital—or the worst-case scenario: dead—then now is the time to back out. Everybody going into this needs to be one hundred percent on board. We need to be able to rely on that. If this is something you can't do, then please leave now."

Everybody glances around, some seem nervous, some seem pensive, all are nauseous with fear. One guy starts to back away, and before he breaks, he looks askingly at Bobby. Bobby glances to Marcus, who is the founder of the gang, as he makes his way behind the nervous young man. "It's okay, Frankie. I will buy you a beer at the show on Saturday to show you that there are no hard feelings."

Frankie looks down, ashamed. "I'm sorry, Marcus. I just …" and with that he turns and quickly walks towards Broadway. With the green light of the first individual to leave, fifteen or so others follow suit, staring at the soggy ground as they walk away. Part of me is ashamed of my own fear, wishing I could join them, and another part of me is angry that they had taken the out, because I just can't. This is the only chance to prove myself. I find myself getting angry, thinking how others have the option of opting out, but I always feel compelled beyond my will to stay the course.

After the crowd of defectors are out of earshot, Marcus perks up, "Now that the cowards are gone, let's talk strategy," and launches into a long, drawn-out war games session that I can't stay focused on.

Years of getting beat up by my father, years of homelessness, my father's murder, and I have never really thought of the application of violence. But I am now faced with it. What are we about to do? Why are we doing what we are doing? Doesn't this violence just become a cycle? Just as I get dizzy with fear and confusion, I feel a hand on my shoulder. It's Bobby.

Bobby has always been like a big brother to me ever since he first saw me getting my ass kicked for pushing a bonehead into a fountain for handing out white power fliers at a punk rock show. He beat off the boneheads and picked me up off the ground. He bought me food when I had no money to eat. He paid for me to get into punk shows. Bobby is the man I use as my example of how a real man should be: compassionate and loving, but stoic and dangerous.

"You alright, Tugboat? You look upset."

I'm more afraid to tell Bobby that I'm afraid than I am afraid that I'm about to take part in something that could kill me, imprison me, and most definitely alter the course of my life forever.

"I'm fine, man. Just a little on edge, being the small guy and all."

"Well, that is why Marcus and I have a special plan for you. You see, nobody knows who you are. We want you to set it off and then vanish."

Bobby breaks into a detailed plan. Basically, everybody is going to wait around one corner from the venue. I am to approach from the other side, sucker punch the first guy I think I can outrun, and lead him around the corner and directly into the gauntlet of anti-racists waiting for him.

This is not only something I can do, but it also makes me feel valuable, like I am part of the team.

My cigarette shakes in my hand as our large group crosses West Broadway toward the venue and past the awkward stares of traffic and pedestrians. I really hadn't thought what we must have looked like to an unknowing innocent bystander. Tattoo-faced punk rockers with pit bulls. Skinheads with bricks and baseball bats. Guys in track suits and Kangol caps. Unrecognizable figures with every inch of their body covered in black, all except their eyes. We know we are going to war. One can only assume that the rest of Portland can feel the tension emanating from us.

Half of the group lines up against the wall on the north side of the street and the other half against the wall on the south side of the street. This has to be done fast, before the cops get here. We assume they have already been called by a nervous busybody and that they are already on their way. Marcus and Bobby lead me around the block. I smoke a cigarette in what feels like one drag; it doesn't seem like enough. My heart is trying to jump out of my throat, as is my stomach. I just need to get this over with.

As we near the corner, I feel something cold and hard against the palm of my hand. I jump a little and notice that Marcus is behind me trying to put a brick in my hand.

"It will give you a couple of seconds to get out of arm's reach," he says, steadying my arm so he can place the unnaturally red stone in my hand.

If I think about it one more second, I won't do it. Without even peeking to see who is there, I put my bricked hand behind my back and make my way around the corner.

There are four of them outside the venue. One of them has a patch that says "EK," for European Kindred, and I instantly feel at ease with what I have to do. In front of me are four men, a small representation of the possible one hundred inside, who are out to destroy communities and families with their message of racial hatred. My pace quickens. As I near them, I actually overhear, "I can't believe there is no sign of those Antifa bastards. Looks like we might finally be left alone."

Right then, a cop blasts his siren at what I am assuming is a driver. One of the boneheads turns his head (my pace quickens). I see that he is standing outside of arm's reach of the others (my pace quickens), furthest towards the other side of the block (my pace quickens), and closest to my allies in waiting (my pace quickens). The brick feels as if it is an extension of me (my pace quickens), pendulums front (my pace quickens), then back (my pace quickens). Jump. Swing.

+ + +

Existence itself is an act of violence.

+ + +

Summer 2002

My best friend Rodent and I are sitting at the Multnomah Pub, trying to get as drunk as our no-money will allow us, and Cynthia walks in. The sun is shining, making her a silhouette, but her shape, her dreads, and floral dress are unmistakable. Cynthia is a hippy girl who just happens to drink in our local watering hole. We normally don't have any love for hippies, but she has a tendency to get drunk and buy rounds, so we keep her around.

As the door closes behind her and light swarms her face, I see that she has two black eyes, a busted nose, and a number of other nicks and scrapes. Rodent and I mockingly ask her what boxer she said the wrong thing to. Her hands race to her face and she begins weeping uncontrollably. She might be a hippy, maybe she looks down on my friends and me, but she is our classist hippy. She drinks where we drink, and that connects us. With that understanding, Rodent and I rush to her side, as she starts to wobble. Guiding her to an empty seat at our table, we simultaneously ask, "What's wrong? Who did this to you?"

After a few shots of whiskey and a pitcher of beer in front of her, she proceeds to tell us how her boyfriend had beat her up the night before. This is why she came to the bar so early; she's afraid he is going to find her, so she wanted to be where it was safe. She laughs as she admits, "Unfortunately, the safest place for me to be is around you psychopaths," referring to the roughneck punks and skinheads that drink at the Multnomah Pub, like Rodent and me. So, she makes a deal with us. She will buy us drinks throughout the day and into the night, if we would accompany her back to her apartment and stay with her until this "thing" with her abusive boyfriend simmers down. Being the poor, thirsty, and mooching bums that we are, we eagerly oblige her.

And with that, the party commences. How many pitchers of beer, how many shots, how many Merle Haggard sing-alongs later, I'm not quite sure, but we eventually make our way to a different bar across the river. Rodent and I are very excited, because they have dollar twelve-ounce bottles of Pabst Blue Ribbon, which we drink by the bucket load. We're having a great time ruffling the feathers of the middle-class kids from the east side who like to dress as if they are actual punks but know nothing of the culture. Being a black punk rocker often brings Rodent to the center of attention, both good and bad, and he loves shattering all the privileged kids' liberal sentimentality by making blatantly racist jokes and never hiding his over-sexed and lustful intentions with every woman who didn't detest him within seven seconds of meeting him.

Cynthia finds an old buddy at the bar she casually slept with in school and wants to take him back to the apartment to have at it again, before Rodent and I walk in and join the party. (Yeah, we're that drunk.) We are a little worried about the situation but let her go, as she is currently our place to crash indoors, and we don't want to get in the way of her plans. Plus, she could use a piece of ass that wasn't her degenerate woman-beating boyfriend. Unfortunately for Rodent and me, once our calming companion leaves, we are like feral dogs without leashes and quickly overstay our welcome. The locals are getting restless, so we make our way to the bodega to grab forty ounces of malt liquor for the slow walk back to Cynthia's place. Knowing there is a girl with meth and an appetite for more than one man waiting for us is rather exciting. We want to pace ourselves and prepare.

As we walk down Sandy Boulevard, we casually sip our beers, as if it is our birthright. Rodent keeps talking about what we were going to do to the guy when we get our hands on him. We always seem to be talking about the times we did bad things to good people together, or just doing bad things in general, and I am getting kind of tired of it. I want to be respected for being a good guy. I don't want to be feared anymore. And right then we are approached by a guy on a bicycle. I instantly feel uneasy in the presence of this dread-locked individual.

"Hey, you know that bitch Cynthia?" the shadowed cyclist asks us.

Holy shit! It is Cynthia's abusive boyfriend. Somehow, we had stumbled across the one guy whom this whole day of drinking and hanging out with Cynthia was thanks to. I had to play it cool. Rodent and I exchange glances. We had just found the fight we were looking for since our fifth shot of Jameson.

I return his question with another, "Not that hippy bitch that drinks at the Multnomah?"

"Yeah, that's the one. Wait, you guys drink down there—I think I've seen you in there. So, have you seen her?" he asks.

"Nah, I haven't seen her since ..." and the rest of my feigned congeniality is drowned by the breaking of glass across the dreaded face of a misogynist hippy.

My life was built on what seemed an inherent relationship with violence. As much as we sentimentally want to try to condemn all violence, or the abstract of violence, I have learned that violence and the pains that stem from violence are often the catalyst for deeper and more compassionate understandings and perspectives of the world we inhabit. My years as a homeless youth, a gang member, anti-racist activist, a teenage gay-for-pay prostitute, a drug addict, led me to believe one thing, one thing that can't be unlearned: survival is a game of force. This world, this society, is built upon the construct that one can only ever achieve what they are willing to take by force or be broken by. Some may come from a place where this is not a reality, but will eventually succumb to it. Much like the floor of a forest, life itself is dependent upon the destruction and consumption of other life.

LISTENING FOR GOD

We're waiting in line for the answer
we're waiting for anyone   an answer
an answer   some answer   we search for it
     in the empty stares of strangers
in the blue-eyed screams of babies
     the laughter of children
in the too many sandwiches
     in the too long nights
in the red lines of trains going nowhere
     somewhere
     an answer
there is poetry   there is a poem
in the way her see-through skirt
     flows in the breeze   the beige flag of
surrender
the half a top hat   the bicycle helmet
     never worn   still shiny
waiting to bounce off the cold inhumane sidewalk
these bricks   our forefathers
     this city   our nation   our
prison
our cell   our storefront hope for salvation
     Pray to Nike swooshes,
     to taglines,
     & forgiveness.

COIN COUSINS

Turning the coin over
in my hand, the memory comes back.

It was the coin given
to my father by his best friend

during the Vietnam War. It signifies
kinship, or the formation of brotherhood.

A brass coin, engraved Asian writing
with a diamond carved from the middle.

The two men, Steve & my father,
were stationed together on an aircraft

carrier. The Navy made them comrades,
their shared home of Oregon made them neighbors,

the coin made them brothers, the sons
made cousins, & a single lineage

of broken, divided in blood, flowed
from the joining of these two lost boys.

I think of Steve's son, JJ, from time
to time, how we both felt trapped

in that house, how we both sought
to escape. I wonder if his escape

led him down the well-paved road
that my dead-end alley seems to flow

from. I wonder if JJ made his journey
without the terror so characteristic

of mine. I wonder if he can still hear
the doors closing, the tide leaving,

the lonely wail of a foghorn, the single
blast from an unseen gun.

GRESHAM

The mountain is only as majestic as the valley
surrounding its royal feet allows it to be.
A litter of rusting cars, birthed from cracking concrete,
a fistful of mobile homes inhabited by teenagers
collecting hand-me-down strollers & possession charges,
high rises of once low-income housing & factories.
                    Here are a people, broken,
holding up the throne of their mountain
with nothing more than faint memory of what they once
were
to mold them into the shivering denizens they now are,
in the mad, inhumane realm they can only point
& mutter, with chafed & blistered tongues,

Home.

GODSPEED, MY LONELY ANGEL

The machine whirs & spins
& ticks each moment of the space
between the everything. Humming
its crescendo music. The spheres
they call them. A world of worlds
yet to come. Such violets blind each
distended eye. A white beast roams.
We are always guessing. Silly humans.
Every question this pitiful language
can formulate leaves us with one thousand
nine hundred twenty-eight more.
Our sadness is a machine. A tool.
An endless quest for the answer
that cannot exist, as it lies on the tip
of every nose, of every tongue, burning
itself beyond the shadow of our vision.
Everything is hidden. Nothing is hidden.
We are only ever allowed to sing as we
are told to. To dance as commanded.
This is the ball. At the stroke of midnight.
Remove the mask. Kiss me. As
we fall backwards though time.

CAMPBELL IS NO LONGER
CALIFORNIA

for Danny

Bullet holes in capillaries
bled his hands into hammers
of swollen embrace. We sang
under stars that made us
Hollywood Strip saints.

The painkiller appeared
as a rooftop screaming,
leaving us to seek our up-
side down reflections
of spoons & zip-tie tourniquets.

The rest are dead
or headed for Chicago,
on the backs of empire builders.
Empires crafted from tears
that can only be described
as the humane inside us all,

that we keep searching
our veins for
under the doo-wop moonlight.

IT ALL DISAPPEARS

My cat has gone blind in one eye.
With his good eye squeezed
shut, he cries,

staring at the nothing,
trying to will the front door
into existence.

THE ONLY HOME I HAVE EVER KNOWN: PART III

PRODIGAL SON

After an eight-year personal exile to Boston, I returned to Oregon. I am still unsure as to my reasons for leaving Boston and my growing socially-affluent life as a hip-hop and hardcore punk producer and promoter, but I came back to Portland, nonetheless. As far as I knew, all of my friends were dead, dying, institutionalized, or serving life sentences. Having been orphaned at a young age, I never really connected to my family, yet I found myself living on my mother's couch just north of Oregon City.

Being two years sober, as well as a productive member of society, I had no business sleeping in my mother's living room. I would trek into downtown Portland every day to find reprieve from the chicken coop of a family house I was squatting in. When I first set my newly-developed east coast legs upon Portland soil, I panicked. There was only one place I knew to go. So, I made a beeline for the Seals. Portland was my Hiroshima; it was my Helena. Everything that had ever gone wrong in my life, every evil I had done, stared back at me, and into me, from the reflection off the rainy bricks.

As I approached the corner, I happened upon two of my longest and oldest friends, the Tweeker Twins. They appeared to have grown twice as old than they were because of years of heavy narcotic use, homelessness, violence, and HIV. I greeted two of my closest lifelong friends with a deepening pit in my stomach. I love them dearly, but I felt as if I was just meeting them for the first time. After half a pack of cigarettes and chatting for what seemed like hours, I needed to find a place where I could escape the too-familiar unfamiliarity, so I made my way to a coffee shop I had been hearing great things about. Backspace was an internet cafe in Chinatown. It was everything I had ever wanted in a coffee shop: exposed brick, vaulted ceilings, computers to use, arcade games in the back, bathrooms riddled with graffiti, and a myriad of weirdo artist types with whom I could spend hours debating the ills of the world and literature.

Over the next two years, I found myself involved in the poetry world. I started working as a poetry editor for a literary magazine. I even enrolled in college for the first time in my thirty-one years of life. Applause was thrown my way from the poetry world, the Buddhist world, and the Twelve-step community. Even some of my friends from the streets found me and congratulated me on survival, sobriety, and publishing. I was flying all over the place making new friends of old heroes in the literary underground and the punk world. I was flown to Los Angeles as a Christmas present from an old drinking buddy of mine who had gotten sober and graduated law school. While there, I visited a friend from two prominent Boston punk bands who were living in SoCal at the time. Someone even started filming a documentary about me and the effect of Buddhist mindfulness in the West. I was becoming heavily traveled and accomplished, yet I never got too far from the Seals.

On a weekly basis, I still find myself sitting next to Sammy, drinking my morning coffee, chain-smoking and reflecting on my past. The Seals has become more a mausoleum than a refuge. Every five or six days, I sit on that concrete fountain rising from the red bricks like a church pew and hold a memorial service for my past. Portland was no longer blue collar, as gentrification has given rise to marketable fashion and past times. The locals got scared and moved away. The timber and fishing industry had given way to food carts, obscure comic book stores, and vintage typewriter shops. The heroin and meth that used to flood the streets has been chased into the trailer parks east of the city.

Voodoo Donuts is all the rage, but I remember when they were a shitty donut shop out of a rickety doorway window. I was actually convinced at one point that they were a front for a drug operation, as I could never understand how they stayed open. Now, Voodoo Donuts serves the same donuts, except now they have the corner where Berbati's Pan once stood and a huge neon sign, under which tourists line up for hours in the cold and rain for a donut in the shape of a dick.

The Silverado, best gay-men's bar in the world, was forced to move from the corner of 12th and Stark, along with the rest of the gay men's bars that lined Stark Street downtown. I love that the hotel now sits where once stood the gay bathhouse. If people only knew what happened in those rooms before the cheap remodel.

One of the best punk bars, the Satyricon, is now housing for active drug addicts and alcoholics. Paris Theater, which was one of the only all-ages venues in town, is now a porn theater owned by the City. The gang territory is now the Alberta Arts District, where the white Californians who satellite their Bay Area tech jobs have moved in and raised the property value, displacing over ten thousand black people in ten years.

Everything has changed. The city has become more intolerable than it was when I ran away to Boston. Only the Seals and the ghosts of my dead friends remain. I am not sure if I will remain here in Portland, but the ghosts have. I can hear them whispering every time I pass the courthouse.

BERTILLON SYSTEM

Bertillon measures time
17.11.23.12
each centimeter an expanse of time
since the boy became man

no print of swirl or crevasse
was given prior to a decade
after last century

legion officer became the first
chief of police
anywhere, ever

clint black, blonde hair & stamps give nothing
more to this night
we were supposed to share

no study of syntactical linguistics
surrounding the science of poetics

shot dead was the use of measurement & I just sit, you,
something else
just spanning these eighteen years
since we were both a part of this world

now it is just me
I care not for these odds

neither does the lonely cowboy
sitting upon a prairie
having just cut off
his ear, forefingers, & nose

ARTEM LASSITUDINEM

God bless Flynn, Yahweh,
& all thankless bastards that move;
take heed of the whirlwind,
the desperate, the collision course.

Here: fission, & gold dust,
hustle & hypothermia.

The tanks have been filled
they are empty & taken
given & lonesome.

This is the swan's
funeral procession.

Here is grapefruit
& tokens for the ferryman.

Styx is not an adventure,
nor a finale, but a beginning;
the alpha of coronation & epilepsy.

The twitches scent is gruesome.
If only it would stop here.

The waving flag is a contrast
of cynics' rust & mailbox red.

& the nights frigid chill;
how do all things not rust
in such mundane conditions?

A HOMELESS MAN YELLING IN A DOORWAY CLUTCHING A BOTTLE OF WILD IRISH ROSE

Pay attention not
to the flames that lick his feet
but to the fuel that feeds them.

Eyes of concrete gray
are not cold shallow graves
but the faded film of a life forgot.

RED MOUNTAIN CREEK, TRINITY MOUNTAINS, NORTHERN CALIFORNIA

+ + +

To get to the other side of the creek,
I walk cautiously amidst
a swirling swarm of wasps.
The tornado of buzzing, undisturbed.

I wish all things in life
were so easy.

+ + +

The dragonfly
blazes downstream, searching.
Stopping upon shaded rocks,
to think of the one he left
upstream.

Crying as he flies away,
he cannot see that his tears
create the very creek
he searches, endlessly.

+ + +

The timid trickle of Red Mountain Creek
reminds me of the roaring river I once was.

I once cascaded through towns,

my fists were erosion,
pushing against every surface
till every purity was washed away
in the fury of my tide.

My tongue would whitewater blasphemies
in the city street valleys
between concrete skyscraper mountains,
its echo was thunder.

She told me I was terrifying,
but I couldn't stop.

I pray.
I pray the well of me runs dry.
I pray my spring collapses;
to only let out a trickle of water
for the snakes to find relief
from the mountain summer sun

and stave off my earthquake
just long enough
to find my way to her ocean.

REMAIN TEACHABLE

Fold the corners, fold your-
self into everything you knew
you never could. Follow the corners,
follow yourself into everywhere
you have never let yourself.

Follow your folded corners.
You are every book & underlined passage.
Follow these passages. They
may lead to your end, but where
else might your end lie were you
to not follow yourself into yourself?

Origami is the art of manipulating paper,
building with malleability.
Can you see it?
We are malleable like water;
we are not a mass to amass
yet we can be folded and shaped.

Survival is the art of making
ourselves more malleable
than silly little papers.

SLABTOWN SESSIONS

for Slabtown (RIP)

The beer neon in the middle
of this dimly lit bar is screaming.

Red and white, the colors
of St. George's Cross
which is always unsettling.

A squad of cheerleader-looking,
& sounding, youngsters
sit beneath it cackling three octaves
beyond bearable. Louder

than the screaming sign,
echoing shades of Maggie's
Falklands-incited racism.

I met with a friend today
to print posters for his going
away party. He is already gone.

I stood in the office supply,
ruminating on the decades
of bigotry that felt like it shattered
at the end of our fists.

Who needs apologies,
or excuses? The sign
hanging in the bar
is never silent.

I doubt silence

would shout a farewell
anytime soon.

I never thought acceptance
would ever mean
growing accustomed

& comfortable
to the things that torture us.

THAT FIRST TRAIN

The first time I ever crouched
in the ass of a grainer,
it was all crack, rumble, & wind.
Fourteen years old, burgeoning
street corner hoodlum
complete with mohawk & steel toes.

We laid quiet in the Brooklyn train yard
just south of Portland, Oregon,
waiting for the whistle.
I thought we were waiting
for a boxcar, but when the weight of my pack
moved me towards the train,

I had no time to wonder which one.
Just grab on & dig in. We were
bound for San Francisco.
There was something magical
about the sunset, about the wind,
about living like literary heroes.

In retrospect, I hate freight trains.
It's too cold, too loud to talk
to the nobody I traveled with—
just my brain & my fear & the lonely that echoed
louder than cracking & creaking.

I took to rubber tramping
in two months time & never looked back.
So many chances & state lines,
so many opportunities
to cash in on the sympathy

of strangers. Some nights,

like these, I sit at the coffeehouse
writing these poems, waiting to hear
the whistle. Then it comes.
I hear the whistle & the rumble, & wish
I had somewhere better to be.

A SINGLE HEARTBEAT IN THE SYMPHONY OF COMMERCE

The homeless all have suitcases;
the kind with wheels & a handle
that can be dragged behind them.

Except, on every homeless person's suitcase,
one of the wheels is broken,
so that the bottom of their luggage
scrapes across the brick
giving the erosion of fabric
an unsettling heartbeat.

As they near the street corner, biting
at their own ears, talking to ghosts,
their pace slows to check for traffic.

& as they slow, so does the beat
of their bundled possessions.

There are only so many footsteps
from forgotten a human can take
until they cease being human,
until they cease living

for anything other than the perpetuation
of the corpse of their worth
they drag behind them.

THE ONLY HOME I HAVE EVER KNOWN: PART IV

EPILOGUE: WHEN THINGS ACTUALLY SEEM TO WORK OUT

The day I started this essay, I met with an old friend, Little Jenn. Little Jenn is a girl I met at the Seals in the early '90s. We ran along the same paths of heroin addiction, train hopping, and destitution, but we were never really close. However, when I found her, we both survived and came out on the other side of that life which was supposed to ultimately kill us. She is starting the Masters of Social Work program at Portland State. I left class to meet her at a local coffee shop with my stomach churning. I was about to talk to the person whose success would prove I could never go back to the old life. I could never settle for shooting heroin and living under bridges again. I could never choose to travel to Chicago by way of freight train again. This coffee date would be my rite of passage. I could never turn back to the boy I once was.

When we met, we talked about old friends—who had died, and what the living ones were doing. Who was dying of HIV, who was still strung out, which of the dirtbags became holier than thou and refused to say hello on their way to church. They are a rare few, but they do exist. We talked about old times, about getting pulled off a freight train in Pendleton and who still made it all the way to Milwaukee, Wisconsin, for a music festival. We talked about our friend Bruce who just recently died.

- Were you with us in the Field of Dreams when the car backfired and the cops came?
- No fucking way! What happened?
- They surrounded the field with their guns drawn. We all had to walk out with our

hands behind our heads. My pants kept falling down because KC and I were caught mid-coitus. Anyway, when we got to the street, I noticed Bruce was missing. The cops were being cool. They really liked my "Fuck You You Fucking Fuck" shirt. While they were chatting with us waiting for our names to come back clear, I saw Bruce military crawling from bush to bush. We were all cracking up and the cops thought we were laughing at their bad jokes.

- No shit!?
- When they let us go back to bed, Bruce was hiding in a bush whispering to us asking if the Gestapo was gone.
- Man, I miss him.
- Yeah, me too.
- ...
- ...
- Do you talk to Badger anymore?
- We haven't talked since I fucked Slinky's girlfriend. But he did accept my friend request on Facebook, so, who knows. Maybe I will go down to Ashland to get a tattoo from him.
- What about Buck?
- I actually just got back from his shroom farm in Wyoming. He is all about the ayahuasca these days. Talkin' about moving to Mexico.
- Jesus, who would have thought?

A funny thing happened, though. We started talking about our survival. We talked about our successes. We talked about our hopes. We talked about how fortunate we were to have hopes, and also the capacity to see those hopes manifest. We talked about our dreams and what we wanted out of life. We talked about what we could offer to the world around us. Neither of us expected to live this long, but we sure as hell didn't expect to have conversations involving the actualization of hopes or dreams. Those who come from where we came from are never afforded such luxuries as dreams and aspirations. People like us just died or made due with what would be given us and eroded away. We were only ever supposed to be grains of sand; once used to build a sandcastle, we were supposed to be washed out to sea, drowned and forgotten.

The last thing we talked about was how we felt like outsiders, no matter where we went. We could no longer relate to the world we came from, yet the world we live in now is still so alien. Old punks never assimilate well. We just get washed away in the tide. Yet, we did not. This is both funny and terrifying.

+ + +

It is autumn. I have a book of poetry coming out and Little Jenn is trying to have a baby. Maybe fall doesn't equate all those things I once defined myself as. Maybe fall means new. This must be true. I have become so fluent in change, that change is how I now define myself. Maybe it has something to do with falling from trees and sowing new seeds. Maybe I am just too much of a poet to think clearly. Maybe this is a good thing. Who knows? Ask me next year. I am sure things will be different. Change is something I know well.

SWEET NOTHINGS FOR POETS

for Matthew Dickman

I could be drinking it in, both booze
the young woman with zippers for legs.
Drinking in the conviviality of shots
of Jägermeister & of mumble rap
seemingly more coherent the gnarled mutterings
sloshing between my ears. Drink it all in.
Yet I stare at this page & think of you.
Our shared moment by the canyon
hiding from the crowd in the cloud
of our multicolored taste for American Spirits.
I think of your partner's overalls & how she played
fairy farmer hype-man to the writing workshop
karaoke night, her hair tucked neatly under her cap.
I think of your son & how his blue eyes widened.
How the most beautiful smile I have ever seen
crept across his face—like the rainbow of oil
spreads across puddles of fresh October Portland
rain—the moment our eyes first met. I think
about your brother, whom I have never met.
I wonder if he would approve you calling me brother,
as well as the brother I'll never know.
I could be drinking in life, bubbling through simple-
minded chat with even more simple-minded co-eds.
But instead, I finish my meal. I pay my tab.
Walk across the street to the train stop.
Sit on a bench. Light a cigarette.
Think of you & write this poem

ANOTHER UNWRITTEN LETTER
for Micah

How come I never told you how much I admire you?
The way you plaster every loose-leaf poem
with your bleeding heart. How your sorrow found no
rival
when I told you of the hatred that runs deep under city
streets.

From a trench coat & a trilby to steel-toed boots
& a button-down, you went from boy to soldier
so fast I am still queasy. How could I have warned you

about the gleam of meth in the eye of a knife & how it
siren
sings you into its grip, how the stampede of marching
boots
become the anthem from which my heart still finds its
rhythm,

& the first time we shave our heads & lace up our boots
how boring sex becomes compared to it, how much
more important
it is to receive the hatred of others into our open veins,

than it is to breed—this life is a drug that is not easily
kicked.
Today, this city lauded you a hero & you are. Not for
standing up
for what is right, but seeing the beauty in the world
& throwing it a fucking life preserver.

WITH NO BRIDGES ~ OR ~ FUCK RED HOT CHILI PEPPERS

We climbed into the bottom of the overpass,
a dimension of sepia hues & sharp straight
edges. The only place one learns how car tires
moan. A boy transformed into some mutated
version of man, some daemonic assimilation
of human. Every experience gleaned makes one

more innocent. Every narcotic breath a holocaust.   gon
This was our wardrobe, but no savior lion.   up
Only slave driver witch. A street corner skeleton   up
mouth stretched between both coasts filled   up
with a rainbow of tiny balloons, which we prayed   up
would take us up up up, float us somewhere safe   up
with no bridges. But we're still floating   up

LINES

If I know one thing, it is how to stand
in line. How to wait patiently for whatever
is to come. Whether I am grinding my teeth
or I am not grinding my teeth, I know
how to make my waiting look graceful,
seem transparently buoyant. Stand in line.
Fall in line. Pick up the slack. Tow
the line. Know your place. Take your place.
State your name & rank. Squat. Give two
coughs.
       You see, these lines are mobile prisons.
We are asked to move orderly throughout
our time in these bodies & in these bodies
of collected bodies called communities. But
we could call them units—cells, stockades.
These lines in the banks & in the stores
& in the DMV & in school & in traffic—
these lines are our judgment. If God exists,
then she is our jailor, our warden, hack, screw, bull.

The line moves. I blink. Once for run,
twice for duck, three times for stab
that rat punk behind you.

WINTER QUIETS THE CITY

Steam of fresh blood sizzles
as it falls upon loose dry snow.
The silence of falling snow
only ever breaks with the wail
of sirens. Yet the next blurt
of ambulance ignores our victim
as he stitches himself back together
in the bar bathroom. Still silent.
Still bleeding. The bloody powder
gets buried, along with the crime,
with every falling snow flurry.

INNER CITY INTROSPECTION

Burgundy. I often tell people
my favorite color is burgundy.
However, that is not true.
My favorite color is brick blood—
stain red. After getting bleached
by the sun, red bricks take a burnt
orange hue to them, like blood
stains your shirt during a street
fight. Like blood stains the blood
stained bricks. Like this corner
is your castle & your enemies
can follow a trail of the dead
to your doorstep. Street corner
kingpin they will call you. They
will call you hoodlum, criminal,
monster, or hatred incarnate.
But what else is there these summer
nights full of heat & sweat
& bad ideas? The wine you drink
is the color of the bricks it spills
upon, just like the blood you spill
looks like the only home you've ever known.

KALI YUGA IN DROP D

A mosh pit erupts
rhythm of heartbeat racing,
teeth grinding, joints twisting,
muscles twitching defiantly
to the ballet of hatred & regret
that flows like blood from a VFW
hall in rural upstate New York.
All seems silent, each moment building,
fists clenching, ears ringing
like an open E chord, like tinnitus,
like air raid sirens with no desks
to make believe we will ever be safe
under. Except here
                           in this dimly lit
point between all time & space
waiting for the breakdown. Where we can swing
our contrived Boston accents like Trishul
hoping to tear down the fury of the heavens
with every scream. Multiply a convocation of eagles
by the roar of the deadliest river
& you would still be unable to find
my God's name in the throats of the innocent
while they choke on our fury.
A cry erupts at the stomping of hooves,
the cawing of crows, the striking of lightning
it is in the eye of this storm from which we walk
midst the swirl of hometown & dead
futures. We will walk unscathed
into your little wretched world,
born of sore throats & chaffed tongues.

ALONE ITCHES

The screen flickers. A stone-wash
denim blue bandanna drapes over the lamp
to keep out excess light—shame
comes more standard under halogen at 3am.
A dilapidated junkyard of soda cans, cigarette
butts, & last month's medical bills spills
across the desk like a tidal wave of blind-eye,
a tsunami of keeping-busy-to-keep-the-hurt-out.
He struggles against the temptation of pixels,
but how can he ignore the nostalgia of an age
when he would bend & sweat & twist
& dread the rising sun signaling the night
as *over?* At this station, he grunts & moans
to no one but his twisted body & low hum
of a computer. A machine that makes the alone
go away with the tide of yesterday's refuse.

A REVELATION

Leave us to think of dappled horse chariots

of songs about fathers of purple seaweed waves

sinking into foam crashing waves crashing

against our shores against our bodies

hovering before the end in a halo of disembodied light

angels they'll call us demons to some

to call a calling

to twist into hazy vision of breathlessness

the sound of gulls lapping the beaches

at night, feeding the air whispers threats

of sunrise of the great culling

we hear the horns unmuted blasts from the sky

a voice echoes or maybe it's the crashing

but the echo & silence there seems no relief

from the snarling & the flapping of wings

the wind & the teeth there is blood in the water

& us in the water   & a death in the water

& a death   & the water

HOW OPTIMISM IS ACTUALLY EXISTENTIAL NIHILISM AT THE HEART OF EVERY POET

Walk with me as I recall virility
like the blue breasted song of a meadowlark
blaring & powerful, as my cock once was.
Before this weight, this depression,
the kidney kick of age. Walk with me
as I stumble along the words of songs
long forgotten, anthems of youth
& hope, & everything else which I
no longer have, & everything that makes me
cry when I watch movies. Like a checklist:
"Don't have that." "Will never experience that again."
"I will never come close to even remembering
how any of that feels." & I cry. I cry
for the boy that never got to be, the man
that once was, & bitter morass of flesh
that grips this pen, that writes this poem,
that prays maybe someday someone
will read my poems, & give me
a sympathy blow job.

ABOUT THE AUTHOR

Johnny No Bueno is the author of *We Were Warriors* (University of Hell Press, 2012). He has had poems and essays published in *Criminal Class Review, Present Tense, Unshod Quills*, and *Nailed Magazine*. Co-founder of Boston's Dharma Punx group, Profound Existence, No Bueno has facilitated poetry and meditation workshops at Maclaren Youth Correctional Facility. No Bueno currently resides in his hometown of Portland, Oregon, where he lives with himself and hopes to someday grow up to be a real boy.

by **Brian S. Ellis**
American Dust Revisited
Often Go Awry

by **Greg Gerding**
The Burning Album of Lame
Venue Voyeurisms: Bars of San Diego
Loser Makes Good: Selected Poems 1994
Piss Artist: Selected Poems 1995-1999
The Idiot Parade: Selected Poems 2000-2005

by **Lauren Gilmore**
Outdancing the Universe

by **Rob Gray**
*The Immaculate Collection/The Rhododendron and
Camellia Year Book (1966)*

by **Joseph Edwin Haeger**
Learn to Swim

by **Lindsey Kugler**
HERE.

by **Wryly T. McCutchen**
My Ugly & Other Love Snarls

by **Michael McLaughlin**
Countless Cinemas

by **Johnny No Bueno**
We Were Warriors

by **Isobel O'Hare**
all this can be yours (hardcover & paperback)

by **A.M. O'Malley**
Expecting Something Else

by **Stephen M. Park**
High & Dry
The Grass Is Greener

by **Christine Rice**
Swarm Theory

by **Thomas Lucky Richards**
Thirst for Beginners

by **Liz Scott**
This Never Happened

by **Michael N. Thompson**
A Murder of Crows

by **Ellyn Touchette**
The Great Right-Here

by **Ran Walker**
Most of My Heroes Don't Appear on No Stamps

by **Sarah Xerta**
Nothing to Do with Me

edited by **Cam Awkward-Rich & Sam Sax**
The Dead Animal Handbook: An Anthology of Contemporary Poetry

CPSIA information can be obtained
at www.ICGtesting.com
Printed in the USA
FSHW011950020420
68727FS